7 THINGS TO KNOW ABOUT GETTING MONEY FOR YOUR BUSINESS

7 THINGS TO KNOW ABOUT GETTING MONEY FOR YOUR BUSINESS

Dr. David Doriscar

ELM HILL

A Division of
HarperCollins Christian Publishing

www.elmhillbooks.com

7 things to know about getting money for your business

Published in Nashville, Tennessee, by Elm Hill, an imprint of Thomas Nelson. Elm Hill and Thomas Nelson are registered trademarks of HarperCollins Christian Publishing, Inc.

Elm Hill titles may be purchased in bulk for educational, business, fund-raising, or sales promotional use. For information, please e-mail SpecialMarkets@ ThomasNelson.com.

Library of Congress Cataloging-in-Publication Data

Library of Congress Control Number: 2020901380

ISBN 978-1-400331239 (Paperback)
ISBN 978-1-400331420 (Hardbound)
ISBN 978-1-400331246 (eBook)

CONTENTS

ABOUT THE AUTHOR

D r. David Doriscar is a professional who has had the privilege of working in many different industries both in the private and in the public sectors. After completing a BS degree in computer information system, Dr. Doriscar continued his quest for knowledge by getting a masters of business administration that help him get his foot into the financial industry. Dr. David Doriscar worked as a series three licensed commodity broker investing commodities via the New York Mercantile Exchange and moved up to becoming the managing partner of the commodity investment firm. While at the firm Dr. Doriscar helped the organization reduce turnover by 80 percent and increase the firm's clientele by 40 percent.

Dr. Doriscar's superior training ability and out-of-the-box thinking continued to help his professional endeavors as a sales manager and marketing coordinator, he was able to make significant accomplishments on both roles at a leading diabetic supply company. During his role as a marketing coordinator, his tenacity led him to get 10,000 new prospects for the firm at 70 percent less than the marketing budget, with projected revenues over 4 million dollars in billable earnings for the firm. As a sales manager Dr. Doriscar counted on his superior training ability to help 80 percent of the bottom performing 20 percent of the sales force to improve their sales performance by an average increase of 35 percent within 120 days.

Dr. Doriscar was raised in a community-active family. Being the son of a preacher who did great financial literacy programs for his congregation, Dr. Doriscar felt the call to continue the legacy of his late father by helping to strengthen the growth of the church and the community-based activities. In his quest to continue sharpening his skills to serve the community, Dr. Doriscar decided to work in academia. In his role as a graduate admission adviser and eventually a student success manager, Dr. Doriscar has had the privilege to help individuals looking to change careers and better themselves through education. In his role in the graduate department he has enrolled hundreds of students in diverse graduate programs to help lift themselves to a better future. During this time Dr. Doriscar has sought to further equip himself with more education, earning a postgraduate certificate in applied behavior analysis and a graduate certificate in human resource. Finally, Dr. Doriscar received his doctorate of education in leadership and management. Eventually, Dr. Doriscar resigned at Kaplan University and started Doriscar Capital Group to help businesses and real estate investors receive the adequate funding that may not be readily available through traditional banking measures. With a diverse set of funding options at Doriscar Capital Group, organizations can receive funding to grow or to get capital for a purchase order, instead of waiting for payment in ninety-day increments. Doriscar Capital Group has a network of at least 100 funders that finance projects from microloans to north of 100-million-dollar projects.

Dr. Doriscar is a proud member of the Golden Key Honor Society, and is part of many professional associations like the Organizational

Behavior Management, Academy of Management, and the Society for Human Resource. Dr. Doriscar has founded the nonprofit organization LSC Community Center, where he has partnered with universities, faith-based communities, and other nonprofit entrepreneurial organizations to hold career symposiums within the community. In addition to being the overseer of the Lively Stone Church of Miami and Port Charlotte, he was also a big brother in the big brother, big sister organization, and he loves his experience with that community.

ACKNOWLEDGEMENTS

I would like to first thank God; he has given me amazing grace. The opportunities he has given me goes way beyond what I deserve. There is not a thing that I have accomplished that I can truly say was because of my merit but by his amazing grace. I could never truly repay and thank him adequately for the many blessings he has given. Lord, I also want to thank you for my wife Vania, and my sons Edanne and David. Secondly, I would like to thank my wife Vania Doriscar. Through all the ups and downs, through a bachelor's degree, an MBA, several other intermittent graduate certificates, and finally through my doctorate in leadership and management, you have been a consistent support system. I love you. As of the writing of this book the Lord has given us over fifteen years of a blessed marriage, for which I am grateful. In regards to my parents, my late father is no longer with us for me to witness his hearing of my words of gratitude to all that he has done for our family. Dad, Woolly Doriscar, you have given me an example to work toward. You were a very intelligent man of faith, who was benevolent and giving not only to your family but also the community at large. This example has forever changed my life. Your military-like focus to a purpose-driven life has forever seared in my conscience a desire to live on purpose. I thank you for this in addition to all the sacrifices you have given to your family. To my mother Esther Doriscar, I am thankful that as I write this book you are still with us. I thank you as well not only for the countless times I have been able to count on you for spiritual and natural support, but for what I also learned through your example. You and dad's financial support allowed me to take chances, and know that if you had anything you would help me if I fall. That alone was indispensable to any success I have gained because it allowed me to take chances that would pay off. I also want to thank you for your example because what I didn't get from Dad, I got from you. Dad was always focused on work, but didn't adequately take time to smell the roses and be a great steward of his health. While I learn so much from dad's studious study of both biblical and philosophical subjects, it was your worship that has also been invaluable to who I am today. Watching how you manage how you eat, how you have a regular exercise schedule even in retirement, and the balance by which you carry your life is something that is a goal of mine for my later years. You have given me a desire to grow old that didn't exist prior to me witnessing how well you did it. To my in-laws, I have been spoiled and will forever rank you as the standard by which in-laws should carry themselves. My wife and I would not have made it this far without both of you. To my siblings, I have been truly blessed to have you all. I first thank you for my wonderful niece and nephews. Beginning with my brother Pastor Jude Doriscar. God chose you to be my brother; I really do not know how I can do any of the things I have done without you. We have been such a great team, regardless of the roles in which we are in life. You did such a great job introducing me to many of the things that I am into today. Due to the fact that Dad traveled a lot, my love for music, jazz, and ministry has been something that you introduced me to. Introducing that intellectual curiosity at such a young age is something that I will forever be grateful for. It is truly a pleasure to partner with you in ministry. To my sister Dr. Ruth Cook, thank you for your great example in parenting. You truly have a gift of reaching young people. I still use with my son Edanne the books you use with your daughter. To my oldest sister Dr. Katsia Cadeau, I thank God for you. It is truly a pleasure to partner with you in everything. I still thank God for giving Dad you. When Dad passed away, you took the mantel of ensuring Dad's work continued with me and Pastor Jude. It is such a privilege to have someone like you as a sister. I like to thank my church family Lively Stone Church of Miami and Port Charlotte. God knows that we are truly a family, and all that I accomplish is a big part of your accomplishment. My wife and my church family has been the most consistent in asking me when will I begin to write books. I also like to thank my extended church family in the Body of Christ. Last but not least, I would also like to thank Eric McConell; you have been an awesome support for me throughout the ups and downs in this endeavor.

INTRODUCTION

F irst disclaimer of this book is that I have tried to the best of my abilities to write this for nonfinancial people. I am aware that many of the people who start businesses do not have a background in finance. They are not experts in financial terms. So to the best of my ability I tried to use more common terms when available. I am also aware that this may come at a cost of not using terms that may more appropriately convey the breadth of the topic being explained. However, the trade-off that I'm using is that if you are more advanced, it is easier for you to understand the layman's term than maybe less perfectly fitting to the topic I'm explaining, then it is for someone to understand the complex terminology that may explain in better detail the topic when they are a neophyte.

This book will hopefully have some insights for both people who are currently in need of getting money for their business, as well as people who are in a situation where they currently do not feel like they need any money but would like to be armed with the knowledge that may be useful if they ever did need to consider financing. So let us go on to discuss the seven things you need to know to get money for your business. There are a ton of things that one probably should know that goes beyond the seven that I covered. However, I believe that knowing the seven things will give you a great enough advantage to make informed decisions that will aid in your pursuit of getting funding for your business.

The main way that this book helps you is by informing you the way that many funding institutions look at situations. I have witnessed a fundamental difference in the way a business owner/real estate investor looks at the need for loans and funding, as well as the timing of that quest with how lenders/funders look at the same scenario. The difference has caused many business owners to feel angry when they are denied by a lending institution and take their deposit accounts to other banks as a result. The aim of this book is to bridge some of that gap for business owners and real estate investors. I do owe a great level of gratitude to Doriscar Capital Group, because it is through my experience learning the lending norms of about 100 lenders/funders that has enabled me to witness the glaring divide in perspectives that this book looks to bridge in part.

CHAPTER 1

WHY YOU SHOULD GET IT WHEN YOU DON'T NEED IT

It is better to look for business funding when you don't need the funding, versus when you are in need of funding. This sounds very counterintuitive because if you have a business and things are going great, you do not think there is a need for funding and some people might even feel that this advice is too dependent on a debt-centric philosophy. However, this advice is based upon two very important points.

Number one, you have the greatest leverage to shop for the best rates when you are not in dire need. Banks, funders, or investors are very nervous about lending money to people who need it. As weird as that sounds the concern is the poor choices that put you in a situation where you have a dire need may still be the very same reason why you may default on the loan that they give you, which creates the first dilemma in this book. Many people who feel that they are in a good financial situation will have to go against the instincts to remain in the

1

comfort zone of no action and arm themselves with the needed knowledge that may allow them to enjoy the greatest benefit from being in their good to great situation.

The second benefit in shopping for funding when you don't need it is that you are less likely to use it irresponsibly if you are funded. This is a principle that also applies to personal finances. For example, if you get a credit card with a $10,000 limit. What most people don't understand is that you can use up to 30 percent of that maximum limit before it begins to impact your credit negatively, which means that the $10,000 limit is really a $3,000 limit if you do not want to see any slippage in your credit.

Before one signs up for a line of credit or a bank loan or add to an existing loan, it is understandable to contemplate about whether the business really needs to borrow the money. In such perilous economic times, with rising bills and economic uncertainty, there are many people who choose to stay clear of borrowing money when they believe they have the cash to pay the bills they currently have. It is something that will require someone to understand that situations can change that may also change their calculus. Deciding whether one should be borrowing money is a big decision. There are some critical questions that one should answer before one borrows money, and they include where the money will be spent, whether the business can seek other ways of financing the activities, and if the business can afford to pay back the money that it plans to borrow.

Borrow When Owner Least Expects the Business to Require It

Kassar (2014) advised his readers to only think about borrowing a loan when they least expect the business to need it. While working for a loan brokerage firm, Kassar (2014) had observed many small business owners who on a daily basis are in dire need for business credit, to save their businesses and for their own survival. Kassar (2014) believed that had they called on him much earlier, when at a point when their financial needs were just creeping, applying and securing a loan or a line of credit could have been easy. It is rational, however, that numerous small businesses disregard and overlook the fact that it is even easier to secure a loan or a line of credit when they do not need one, compared to when they are in a dire situation.

Consider an example where at the height of summer and one's own air conditioner gets destroyed. It is going to cost $30,000 to get another, and since it is a hot period it should be procured quickly. This is a moment in time when no thinking is needed or the business will be at risk. When the business has an existing line of credit for such types of emergencies, the business owner can simply write a check and pay at very low interest rates until the individual figures out the long-term plan (Johnson, 2019). If one fails to make that contingency plan, and then one does not have cash on hand, one can be forced to get a really expensive loan where a high interest can be charged for the convenience of getting the funding that quickly. This is what businesses should avoid.

Business owners tend to have short-term memories. When things are moving smoothly, one probably thinks that it will continue on the same path. However, if one were to learn from the events of the last global financial crunch and the subsequent recession, then it is apparent that things can change rapidly and unpredictably. Nothing is immune from shocks. Compare it to a case where a person takes out a life insurance scheme to help them handle things out of unforeseeable situations, and hence business owners should have lifelines for their entities. The most successful business owners expect the possible problems down the road and make plans accordingly before they hit the business (Debt, 2019).

At this juncture, the entrepreneurs know that they are in a good position to borrow when things are quiet. When the business is moving in the right direction, it is time to examine the contingency plan options. When the cash flow is sound and it is increasing, lenders will be more inclined to give the business funds and even at the best interest rate. Overdrafts might be lifesaver in case of unforeseeable emergencies or during the troughs. Even though there might be some small expenses to obtain a line of credit, when it is procured, one can only pay it if it is used.

For a business with accounts receivable and the industry is indicating growth, and the business has a good credit, then the business is in a great position to obtain credit or even a high line of credit at a great rate (rate that favors the borrower, not the creditor). With a firm that is generating positive income, the owner can be confident that it will also be able to repay the loan, which is something that aids firms and business owners to feel at ease.

There can be cases and situations when the business owners know that they are at a bad position to borrow. On the flip side of the coin, when one waits until they are not able to make their payroll or are not able to pay for the lease, it will be much more problematic to obtain any sort of loan because lenders and even shylocks can be hesitant to advance a loan to a firm that is at the risk of not becoming a going concern anymore, or even being declared bankrupt. When the business owner is desperate, his options decrease and one can be stuck with a high interest credit and short amount of time to repay it, and this leave the business back where it began just some few months ago. It occurs when firms can get drawn into the traps of short-term loans renewals that they have problems moving out of it and at the rates that they struggle to repay. For most business owners, this lifesaver loan can be avoided if the loan is taken when the business is not in dire need of it, and it can repay the loan back with much ease.

The bottom line on borrowing has little to do with one's relationship with a bank or other factors. When a lender assesses a credit application or some line of credit request, the only issue they are drawn to is whether the business can repay the loan and make payments within the agreed timeline. This doesn't mean that a relationship can't help if the fundamentals of the application are strong (revenue and credit demonstrate the loan could be repaid) and the business is the type of business the bank likes to fund. For example, at Doriscar Capital Group I remember sending a client's file to one of my funders and was able to get the client a letter of intent within three days. What made this remarkable is that the client went to over fifteen banks and had their credit pulled over fifteen times prior to my involvement. A great part of that was because the fundamentals of the application was strong, but more importantly my relationship with the banker gives them confidence that when they get a file from me it usually is in the area that they have an interest in. When a business is already having some turbulent times when trying to make an application for a loan, the business might look like a bad credit risk (Amit and Zott, 2015). The lender may be concerned that even with the credit advance, the borrower would not be able to generate sufficient business and cash fast enough to repay their credit advance on time.

The solution to this problem before the business digs itself into a deeper hole is to seek credit when it does not need it and then repay the credit to create a good credit history. Thereafter, the business can borrow a little money and then repay it. If the business has established some line of credit, it can always borrow against the good credit history and repay the loan on time, and then seek for marginally larger line of credit. Remember that the objective is to get the business to the point where it has sufficient credit available to carry it through rough moments or help the business through growth spurts.

Reference List

Amit, R. and Zott, C., 2015, "Crafting business architecture: The antecedents of business model design," *Strategic Entrepreneurship Journal*, 9(4), pp. 331–50.

BDC, 2019, "7 deadly sins in borrowing money for your business," (Online). Available at: Hyperlink: https://www.bdc.ca/en/articles-tools/money-finance/get-financing/pages/7-sins-borrowing-money-business.aspx" https://www.bdc.ca/en/articles-tools/money-finance/get-financing/pages/7-sins-borrowing-money-business.aspx [Accessed 26 Sep 2019].

Debt, 2019, "Consumer Credit & Loans," (Online). Available at: Hyperlink: https://www.debt.org/credit/loans/" https://www.debt.org/credit/loans/ [Accessed 26 Sep 2019].

Johnson, H., 2019, "How to decide whether you should use a credit card or a loan to borrow money," [Online]. Available at: Hyperlink: https://www.businessinsider.com/borrow-money-credit-card-or-personal-loan?IR=T"https://www.businessinsider.com/borrow-money-credit-card-or-personal-loan?IR=T [Accessed 26 Sep 2019].

Kassar, A., 2014, "The Absolutely Best Time to Borrow Money," (Online). Available at: Hyperlink: https://www.inc.com/ami-kassar/best-time-to-borrow-money.html, https://www.inc.com/ami-kassar/best-time-to-borrow-money.html (Accessed 26 September 2019).

CHAPTER 2

WHY YOU SHOULD GET THE MAXIMUM POSSIBLE

Try to get the maximum amount of capital available regardless of the amount of capital you think you need. There are many reasons why this is a great idea, but I will mention a few. One primary reason it is a great idea to always accept the maximum number you approved for is because it looks better on your credit when you do not use anywhere near your maximum limit. It is better to get more than you need and still not use what you don't need to use, but at least you know that it is available. There is a term called credit utilization ratio. It basically looks at how close to the maximum limit you are using. Consequently, if you get more funding than needed and not go near the limit, it will be beneficial in terms of giving you an acceptable credit utilization ratio.

Many people may argue that credit utilization ratio is something that is significantly more important for personal loans than business loans. However, most small business owners understand that almost all lending institutions require personal guarantees, where personal credit and personal taxes are also reviewed in addition to the corporation's financials for funding decisions. Another point to consider is the one of many stories people have heard where someone was originally approved for a certain amount but decided to take less than that amount, and when they realized that they needed more the bank would no longer approve the original amount. In a perfect world we would always be 100 percent accurate on the full extent of capital needed without anyone causing delays or problems that can influence the amount of capital needed. However, since we do not live in a perfect world, there is a chance that we could find ourselves in a situation where we need more capital than anticipated, which is why I advocate choosing the better of two imperfect situations. As a result, it is better to have the capital and not need to use all of it, than need capital and not have it.

Although most of the previous paragraphs addressed businesses that are more seasoned that also happen to be in a good financial situation considering debt funding and says very little on equity funding, I also wanted to make sure that I address as wide a group as possible. So I will now also address some of the newer businesses that may not be as seasoned in their industry that may even be considering equity financing since it may be too early to be considered for debt funding. This principle of getting the maximum amount of funding in terms of equity should not be sought by any means. There are many situations where the cost of getting the maximum amount of equity funding outweigh the benefit of seeking it. However, I may mention a few things that makes getting the maximum amount of funding beneficial to the new business whose financial situation is not as well placed in the early years. This principle is also applicable when referring to seed money that can be given through VCs to startups. The next several paragraphs will address the benefit of taking the maximum amount of funding that is more geared toward equity versus debt. However, as mentioned earlier I am of the belief that getting the maximum amount of funding even in debt gives the business owner the most amount of flexibility and leverage to face the unexpected challenges that may arise out of their business.

Numerous startup entrepreneurs often face a dilemma when deciding on the amount of seed funding required to kick start their intellectual property. There exist conflicting opinions regarding this vital issue, some advocating for one to go for a relatively lesser seed funding amount than they actually need. Others are of the opinion that accepting the maximum amount of seed funding available guarantees more advantages as compared to deliberately taking a lower amount of funds. Both sides present solid explanations as well as reasons why it is important for their line of reasoning. That said, however, accepting the maximum amount of funding promises considerably more advantages for the startup as compared to deliberately accepting a lesser amount even when one qualifies for more funding. In light of this then, my objective is to shed more light on why it is advisable to accept the maximum amount of funding. I will discuss the various reasons why more capital is better in the following sentences. Now some people are naturally wired to always accept the most given to them, so my explanations on this point is not needed. However, there is a considerable number of people who believes it will demonstrate greater virtue to not accept the greatest amount, and they feel that added brand building virtue will benefit them in later rounds of funding. My objective is not to say that this mind-set is always incorrect, but to point to many reasons why in some instances it could put a business at a disadvantage.

Combined with the fact that this behavior, which maybe virtuous to some, is not always rewarded in the business world. So if you are of the mind-set to take less, I will feel that I accomplished my goal if you at least consider the pros and cons prior to making a decision, regardless of what decision you make.

Maximum Capital Allows for the Maximum Achievement of Goals and Milestones

New businesses face numerous challenges as well as setbacks when trying to penetrate their particular markets. The challenges may include stiff competition from competitors, lack of knowledge, lack of skilled labor, and lack of operating funds, among others (Cavalieri, 2016). To add on this, the business has to efficiently set its goals and milestones that it aims at achieving, both on the long term and on the short term. This means that the entrepreneurs may have limited knowledge of the future challenges that may arise and oftentimes employees without the adequate experience on the various challenges that may affect them, combined with the task of trying to accomplish their goals. Accepting the maximum amount of funding in such a scenario would ensure they have enough capital to effectively accomplish all the goals and milestones they set aside for a particular financial period even if some unexpected challenges arise. In addition, maximum funding can aid in avoiding the numerous challenges and setbacks; for instance, it can help in funding marketing campaigns that would potentially be effective in dealing with immediate competition. That said, however, entrepreneurs should balance on the level of dilution when accepting maximum funding, but it should not be a deterrence to accepting the maximum amount of funding available.

Maximum Funding Allows for Raising for the Next Fiscal Round

Financial rounds for businesses are often characterized with intense financial turbulence that result in many of the businesses going under in extreme cases. This is usually due to the financial constrains in the initial financial periods. The financial constrains often limit for strategic planning of available funds for next the financial rounds, as the entrepreneurs become bombarded with many setbacks all at once and fail or neglect to plan for strategic planning. With maximum funds, however, it is possible to plan for the next financial rounds, thus ensuring business continuity. Ideally, economists advocate for planning the next round for businesses to be done for around eighteen months. With the maximum amount of funding, this allocation is achieved efficiently.

Accepting the Maximum Funding Could Increase a Business's Worth

With maximum funding, it is possible to acquire the best technology and assets for the particular market segment while still having and attracting the best skilled workforce. Acquisition of the best technology and skills enables speedy achievement of the laid-down goals and objectives. This in turn creates a solid and positive reputation for the business, consequently enhancing its worth as a go-to firm for the particular service or product the organization offers. The positive reputation created has an effect of enhancing the business name, which is an important parameter in the science of business valuation (Trugman, 2016). Additionally, accepting the maximum funding available communicates that the investors have a strong investment as well as intrinsic values for the business. This further amplifies the value of the business, in that it reflects that all the stakeholders are significantly invested in ensuring the success of the business in the long term.

Accepting Maximum Funding Enhances a Company's Return on Equity

Some may argue that the more the funds accepted, the more the time taken on return on equity and the subsequent interests incurred (Anwar, et al., 2018). While this may be true, the maximum funding essentially means more money available for business execution. Many argued that *Amazon* was not fiscally responsible in terms of the amount of money it gathered and invested into the execution of the business, but that investment has more than paid off in the long run. One of Jeff's strategies was to purposely have low profit margins so that he wouldn't attract too many competition (Mohammed, 2018 https://medium.com/@shahmm/how-did-amazon-build-its-sustainable-competitive-advantage-88cfee7fe2c8). In essence then, the more funds available can be utilized by the business to fast-track major business operations such as marketing, enabling strategic acquisitions, product design, beta testing, and the eventual rolling out to the target markets of new products and services. All these business operations need funding and are essential for the success of any business venture. With enough funding, it is possible to perform all of the operations without leaving out any of them. More funds ensure all of the above operations are carried out in a speedier manner, resulting in the firm's break-even period being enhanced and reduced.

Accepting Maximum Funding Enhances a Business's Current Ratio

A business's current ratio aims at evaluating to what extent a business is able to take care of itself over the next fiscal period. The current ratio is calculated by dividing a business's current assets contained in the balance sheet with current liabilities, also contained in the balance sheet's liabilities section. It measures if a firm possesses optimal resources for sustaining itself over a financial year (Boyas and Teeter, 2017). When an entrepreneur accepts the maximum amount of funding available, it directly increases the business's available resources, which are essential for sustaining it over the financial year.

Reference List

Anwar, S., Fathoni, A., Gagah, E., 2018, "ANALYSIS OF THE EFFECT OF CURRENT RATIO, TOTAL TURNOVER ASSETS, DEBT TO EQUITY RATIO AND NET PROFIT MARGIN ON CHANGES OF PROFIT WITH ON EQUITY RETURN AS INTERVENING VARIABLES ON PHARMACEUTICAL COMPANIES LISTED IN INDONESIA STOCK EXCHANGE (BEI) 2013–2017 PERIOD," J. Manag. 4.

Boyas, E., Teeter, R., 2017, "Teaching Financial Ratio Analysis using XBRL, in: Developments in Business Simulation and Experiential Learning: Proceedings of the Annual ABSEL Conference."

Cavalieri, S., 2016, "The role of 3Ts factors in the birth, development and success of a startup."

Drehmann, M., Illes, A., Juselius, M., Santos, M., 2015, "How much income is used for debt payments? A new database for debt service ratios," BIS Q. Rev. Sept.

Trugman, 2016. *Understanding Business Valuation: A Practical Guide to Valuing Small to Medium Sized Businesses*. John Wiley & Sons.

CHAPTER 3

THE DENIAL OF THE QUALIFIED

People with good to great businesses may also be denied by some lending institutions even when they have good to great credit. The main reason why this happens is because the majority of funders or investors are very niche in the way that they fund projects or businesses. This is the reason why your local bank has probably told you that they will not fund or finance your business in spite of the fact that you have banked with them for years and they may know of your financial viability. The main motivation for banks to be this narrow in scope is to mitigate risk of default. Consequently, most funding consideration doesn't involve a lot of in-depth look at how well your business is running if it does not fit the niche that your bank or lender prefers to lend to. This is why people hear stories like when Magic Johnson had to go to several banks before one of them would invest in his business plan. One way that Doriscar Capital Group have helped many clients in this arena is that we have relationships with approximately 100 different lenders, with their preferences organized so that when the lender hears from us, they know that we are sending them something that is close to their niche, which has the added benefit of getting the client closer to yes in a more efficient way, juxtaposed to walking to each bank and hoping that your good business fits that bank's lending preferences.

Over the years, the dynamics of lending institutions have changed drastically. Back then, lending institutions were a bit generous with the way they offered credit to borrowers. In recent times, however, the trend has changed, where more and more people are denied funding by the various institutions even when they qualify for the different loans. This phenomenon has been attributed to the lending institutions being niched about how they offer loans. This phenomenon has resulted in many people being denied funding on the grounds of their purpose for the loans being outside the lender's niche. The institutions have adapted to changing economic trends by reorganizing into a niche-based lending system, with an objective of minimizing their overall risk of default by the lenders. This way, they specialize in a particular niche and do not get burdened by trends from different niches (Warren, 2016). This section of the book aims at discussing the niche-lending phenomenon. In addition, Doriscar Capital Group's efforts on offering borrowers insights to navigate niche banking will be discussed.

What Is Niche Lending?

Niche lenders essentially specialize in a single-market segment and normally have a unique product that they offer to their target-market segment. For instance, some lenders only offer loans that are to be channeled into green energy products, technology-related startups, or toward medical research ventures (Kamruddin and Sultana, 2018). To the lending institutions, the specific product that they offer is their specialty or niche. Niche markets, on the other hand, are specific market subsets on which the individual products are focused. Thus, market niches define the specific features of products that are designed to satisfy needs of specific markets. For instance, production quality, price range, and product demographic. Niche lending is often the reason why various people are denied credit even when they are qualified for the amount, and in some cases are even members of the institutions for long periods of time. A good example is when the legendary Magic Johnson had to seek funding from numerous lending institutions with no success.

Types of Niche Lending

Lending institutions may employ a variety of niches in optimizing their operations. One of the ways they achieve this is through geographical niches. As is suggestive of the name, institutions that employ this type of niche confine their services or product to a specific geographic area. This type can especially be beneficial to borrowers who opt for face-to-face interactions with the lending institution's staff (Graham, n.d.). The relatively low customer base characteristic of this type offers borrowers more attention from the institutions. In borrower niches, the lending institutions specialize in a selected customer group with a clear membership organization that defines their niche. For instance, an institution may focus on first-time home buyers. In philanthropic niches, lending institutions opt to serve particular causes that are often geared toward achieving a community mission. An example of this is the Cherokee Nation's housing project, aimed at providing locals with decent housing. Product niches are arguably the most common, where institutions identify a specific venture that they then lend to customers.

Advantages of Niche Lending

A modern-day adage has it that "in trying to market to everyone, you will market to no one." This simple quote has resonated with numerous lending institutions, as they have made it their foundation in formulating their marketing strategies for their products. Narrowing down on a niche has been linked to offering the individual institutions a competitive edge over rivals, consequently increasing the institutions' eventual bottom lines. When a lending institution identifies a particular niche, relationships with borrowers is enhanced, thus reducing the risk of default cases. As such, an institution can hire staff that is highly informed in the particular niche, resulting in borrowers' experience being seamless, all-round, and informed. In addition, having a niche helps the lending institutions in reducing cost, a factor that results in the generation of more income since specialization enables better as well as more focused resource allocation. The optimization by lending institutions saves the companies and customers time since they know where to seek their loans for their businesses.

Doriscar Capital Group

Doriscar Capital Group understands that many organizations have preferences, and it does not try to change the organization's preference. Rather, it studies each lender's preference and tries to direct traffic based upon that lender's preferences. This is beneficial in two ways. One, it allows the lender to feel confident that when they get a file from Doriscar Capital Group it is already in their niche. Two, it allows the business looking for the loan to get responses more efficiently. Lenders who have confidence in the one sending the file usually acts more aggressively when they know they will not be wasting their time reviewing something that is not in their niche.

Reference List

Doriscar Capital Group, "Business-to-Consumer Finance," 2019.

Graham, S., n.d. "Narrowing your focus can open doors to new opportunities 2."

Kamruddin, S., Sultana, A., 2018, "DIFFERENTIATED BANKS–A STUDY OF PAYMENT BANKS AND SMALL FINANCE BANKS, in: TWO DAY NATIONAL SEMINAR GST AND DIGITAL ECONOMY-IMPLICATIONS ON TRADE AND COMMERCE," p. 93.

Warren, W. S., 2016, "The Frontiers of Peer-to-Peer Lending: Thinking About a New Regulatory Approach," *Duke Tech Rev* 14, 298.

CHAPTER 4

HOW KNOWING WHY YOU NEED IT MAY HELP YOU GET IT

Understanding the reason you need funding may help in strategizing which type of funding you should be seeking. There are many reasons why people may need funding. I will mention below three that may be looked at positively by some funders:

A. Starting your business:

One very important thing that everyone needs to know when starting a business and looking for funding is that money brings money. The number one reason why companies fail is because they underestimate the amount of capital they will need. So organizations that provide funding would like to know that the applicant have adequate personal cash on hand, not only for the 20 percent down payment but also additional savings, which is why many lenders want to consider the personal financial health of the applicant. Oftentimes they review that with a personal financial statement, often referenced as a PFS. The purpose of looking at this is to understand what current living expenses the business owner has so that they can estimate how much proceeds the owner may take from the business for living expenses. It may also explain to the funding organization if there are any additional assets, liquid or not, that the business owner may use in the quest for furthering the business.

B. Getting capital to meet the demands of your growing business:

Many times businesses can experience a growth in terms of demand for their products and services and find that they do not have the current finances needed to try to meet the demand of their customers. This can be an extremely stressful situation because one may feel that they have done everything right, but not having the funding needed to meet an increase in demand can bring some discouragement to a business owner. Oftentimes traditional banking methods may be a challenge in some of these situations. One example that many people have witnessed during this phenomenon is on the popular show *Shark Tank*, where businesses are forced to give away significant equity in order to reach the aim of funding the increased demand.

C. Getting funding to meet a purchase order from a client:

Sometimes businesses just get one big purchase order that can significantly increase their revenues that they are hoping would be the beginning of a trend. Although it may be the precursor of businesses to come, many businesses are faced with the financial challenges of trying to meet that need for the purchase now, and do not see what to do when there isn't a family member or friend who can write a check for them. In addition, many banking institutions may want to wait for the business to demonstrate that this opportunity will be the new reality prior to strongly considering funding the business.

In each of these instances above, there is a different set of strategies and things to consider. If you are starting a business, most entrepreneurs have to either self-fund, get family or friends to fund, or get their funding from a venture capitalist. I will assume that most people reading this book may want to know how to get the funds outside the self, family, and friend zones. So that will leave venture capitalists and traditional lending options to be discussed.

Venture Capitalist

From a historical perspective, venture capitalism has not been a business area that has benefited many startups. In the United States, private equity traces back its roots to over a hundred years. However, recent years saw a considerable burst in private equity as well as venture capitalism as we know it presently. This said, however, many businesses do not get funded by VCs. In the years before the present century, it is hard to conclusively determine how small business as well as startup founders got funds from venture capitalists. However, if fundable statistics are anything to go by, then it is safe to state that an extremely small percentage of startup ventures do actually receive funds from venture capitalists. According to the statistics, only about 0.05 percent get VC funding. Startup founders have to get personal loans from other sources to boost their ventures. This has been the trend over the years since the wake of the present century. In the following sections, this book will further discuss how hard it is to get VC funding, and especially more challenging if one is either a female or a part of a minority group.

The question pertaining to whether to go for VC funding or not comes down to a personal decision. On one hand, a startup founder may desire to break even in a short time and thus look for external funds from a venture capitalist. In such a case, the founder has to let go of a part of their business ownership, thus losing some of the stake to the funding VC. On the other hand, a founder may want to retain autonomy for their startups and thus opt to scale organically (Madden, 2018). In this case, the founder may experience difficulties along the way for lack of adequate funds. Thus, VC funding has its advantages. Startup founders have embraced funding, pushing it to an all-time high of $155 billion as of 2017, according to KMPG projections and statistics. This notwithstanding, it is worth noting that it is extremely difficult to land VC funding, as only 0.62 percent of businesses receive the funds. The odds are even worse if a founder is a woman or is a minority.

Venture capitalists deals often dominate headlines with the huge amounts of capital that they pump into startup ventures. One may think that a huge chunk of the startups swims in the stated huge amounts of funds, but the narrative is extremely different from what is depicted in the news channels. According to fundable, the cases in news headlines are a deliberate "big sticker investments" by the venture capitalists, aimed at enhancing their image. The in-depth scrutiny of startups together with founder scrutiny eliminate a large number of startups from receiving funding from the VCs. Consequently, over 57 percent of the founders have to use personal credit to obtain loans, while around 38 percent have to rely on close friends or family for credit to kick-start their startup ventures (Entis, 2013). Among the reasons that VCs cite for rejecting numerous startups are: a venture being in the wrong geographical area, a venture being in the wrong stage of growth, being in a niche that VCs are not interested in, slow growth, and lacking proper management. Often, a combination of these issues results in large numbers of startup ventures being denied funding.

In addition, women and minority business owners are getting an even smaller piece of the pie, something that is almost nonexistent. So if you are reading this book, this information is to let you know that VC funding is a very difficult task. In truth startup is the most difficult way to get funding out of the three scenarios mentioned above. There is one last way that people often attempt to get funding, and that is through a traditional bank loan. Most startups are not approved for a loan. The exception to this general rule is that I have seen franchises and business purchases get funding at a greater percentage than traditional startups. The reason that I believe that funders have been more open to considering a franchise or business purchase is because it is a proven system that has worked repeatedly. So many lenders may feel that there is less risk in funding a franchise. The new entrepreneurs that I have seen with the greatest amount of success getting funding is people who are buying a business. These are usually the easiest to get funded, due to the fact that there is usually the one thing that all lenders want to see: history. They could look at tax returns, they could look at profit and loss statements. There is data, so that they could plug into their formulas and find ways to mitigate the risk.

Being female can result in one being denied VC funds. In one example, Katrina Lake, CEO and founder of Stitch Fix, has come face-to-face with this inequality (Morgaine, 2017). Race is another major factor upon which founders are denied funding by white male VCs. The situation only gets worse when a founder is female and a minority. In 2018, over $85 billion were given out to startups by VCs. Out of that amount, only around 2.2 percent went to women founders. Worse still, only around 1 percent of that total amount was given to women of color founders (Zipkin, 2018). In her interview with VCs, Melissa Hanna recalled how they were overly concerned about her academic credentials. At the time, she thought it was standard operating procedure, due diligence kind of scrutiny, only to learn that it was due to her being female and black.

As of now, there are around 1,500 African-American startup founders in Silicon Valley. This translates to only 2 percent of the startup founders belonging to a minority group. An African-American founder by the name of Matt Joseph recalled the time when he needed to raise funds for his Locent IP, a startup providing businesses with text-marketing services, to no success, despite having an impressive resume (O'Brien, 2016). In his string of tweets and posts that he went ahead to post on *Twitter* and *Facebook*, respectively, Matt Joseph referred to the behavior of the dozen VCs as "pattern matching." In his view, VCs like to fund businesses that remind them of past successes, such as that of *Facebook*'s Zuckerberg. In the case of Matt Joseph, this meant being matched with rappers and athletes. One of the venture capitalist was even bold enough to bring up Nas, a rapper turned VC. For Joseph, he is adamant that race is still a major impediment toward getting funding from the VCs. Matt Joseph went to Princeton and earned his JD and MBA from UCLA, and was backed by Y combinatory, which is an elite network for entrepreneurs and their businesses (https://money.cnn.com/2016/03/20/technology/y-combinator-locent-matt-joseph-race/index.html). His point was not of VCs being racist but bias because they are looking for pattern matching, which many of them noticed that he doesn't look like Mark

Zuckerberg, which is also impacting the subconscious bias against a minority entrepreneur such as himself. There has been some significant effort in addressing the bias in the VC community in a number of ways, but the point is that even without bias a very small percentage of startups gets funded.

Meeting the Demand for Growth and Purchase-Order Funding

I want to address the remaining two reasons why businesses look for funding simultaneously. In terms of if the business has a growing demand that they need capital for, or if they get a big order from Walmart or a really big customer and they do not have the funds to tackle that will be addressed. Another reason why businesses find themselves needing finances is because of an uptick in demand. Although this is a good situation, it could be pretty frustrating if you notice that people want your product and services but you do not have adequate capital to produce the services or products that your customers desire. Many times people see examples of this on the show *Shark Tank*. On numerous occasions, companies have orders that they can't fulfill without an influx of capital. In some cases, businesses have the capital to actually produce the services or products but it puts them in a very precarious financial situation. Some financing options for businesses in this situation are what we call factoring and purchase-order financing. Although there is no abundance of companies that provide this type of funding, but if you find a lender that does this type of funding it would solve this particular problem without you having to give up all your operating income to fulfill an order. Factoring is when you have performed a service, you have billed for it already, but are in the process of waiting for the actual payment. Sometimes big contracts make you wait sixty days, ninety days, or even longer. If you are able to show a factoring lender your services that you completed, they are usually able to pay you anywhere from 60 to 90 percent of what you are waiting for. Purchase-order financing is even harder to find, but some organizations will also look at the purchase order given and make a determination on whether they will finance that purchase order for you. Doriscar Capital Group has a number of lenders that will work with some of these opportunities.

Reference List

Entis, L., 2013, "Where Startup Funding Really Comes From," (Infographic) [WWW Document]. *Entrepreneur*. URL https://www. entrepreneur.com/article/230011 (accessed 11.24.19).

Madden, D., 2018. "Is It Time to Raise VC Funding? Ask Yourself These 4 Questions to Find Out," [WWW Document]. *Inc.com*. URL https://www.inc.com/debbie-madden/4-reasons-you-dont-need-vc-money-for-your-startup.html (accessed 11.22.19).

Morgaine, B., 2017, "Venture Capital Funding and the Sexism You Can't Quite Prove," [WWW Document]. Bplans Blog. URL https:// articles.bplans.com/venture-capital-funding-and-the-sexism-you-cant-quite-prove/ (accessed 11.21.19).

O'Brien, S.A., 2016, "Black entrepreneur to investors: Stop pretending like race isn't an issue," [WWW Document]. *CNNMoney*. URL https://money.cnn.com/2016/03/20/technology/y-combinator-lo-cent-matt-joseph-race/index.html (accessed 11.22.19).

Zipkin, N., 2018, "Out of $85 Billion in VC Funding Last Year, Only 2.2 Percent Went to Female Founders. And Every Year, Women of Color Get Less Than 1 Percent of Total Funding," [WWW Document]. *Entrepreneur*.   URL   https://www.entrepreneur.com/article/324743 (accessed 11.22.19).

CHAPTER 5

WHY SO LITTLE OR
SO MUCH INTEREST?

What determines the interest charged? Although there is a lot of diversity into what different lenders consider when deciding the niche areas that they decide to play in, one will find out there is a lot more continuity in determining the risk. That basically means that two lenders may agree on your risk profile, and one takes you and the other doesn't for the reasons mentioned earlier concerning whether or not it is in the area that they would like to play in.

However, many people's understanding of what determines the amount of interest charged is wrong because they are not looking at this from a lender's perspective. There is no moral arbiter in terms of interest, just the calculation of what the risk profile is, and what amount of interest would justify that risk level. This is why I tell people that their situation usually has more to do with the interest they pay than the actual lender. The best example I can use for interest is the way you invest for retirement. If you have a financial adviser, one of the first questions they ask you is, "Are you looking to invest in something with a higher return and higher risk, or something safer with lower return?" Usually, the advice given is that the younger you are, the higher risk/return one should seek. The older you get the more one should be changing to a lower risk, lower-return investment choice. Well, in the verisimilitude of the way you approach your investments is the same way that lenders approach lending you the funds needed for your business. If you are a low risk, then you would most likely be eligible for a lower interest loan and vice versa. Your risk is determined by the three C's: credit, collateral, and cash flow.

Essentially, interest rates are the costs charged after borrowing money by the lenders. On the lenders' perspective, interest rates are a sort of compensation for the actual service as well as the risk of loaning money. In both extremes, interest rates ensure that the economy is kept in motion through encouraging people to spend, lend, and borrow. This said, however, interest rates almost always keep on changing, with different kinds of loans requiring different interest rates from others. Whether one is a borrower, lender, or both, it is imperative to have some bit of comprehension underlying the reason why different loans attract different interest rates. This chapter aims at reviewing the various determinants that lenders take into account when calculating the amount of interest to charge a borrower.

As rule of thumb, lenders will usually first determine the level of risk a borrower poses to their loaned finances. One example in the inverse, when investing in a retirement investment portfolio, a young investor would be considered for a high risk and high return investment in comparison to an old investor, who is in most case advised to opt for low risk and low return investment. The same holds when calculating the amount of interest rates to be charged by lenders. A borrower with a relatively low level of risk is considered for a low interest loan, while a borrower with a relatively high risk level will automatically be charged more interest. The rationale behind this is that for a borrower with a high risk level, they pose a relatively high default risk, hence the high interest rate. On the other hand, a borrower with a low risk level will most likely be not a significant risk to default remittance to the lender, therefore being charged a relatively low interest rate.

This notwithstanding, lenders employ other major factors when deciding on the amount of interest rates to charge borrowers. The three C's is a trifecta often employed by lenders in calculating interest rates. The three C's model represents credit, cash flow, and collateral. Together, these factors are scrutinized deeply by the lending institutions. In so doing, different borrowers are classified under different risk levels, hence the different interest rates. This model has been adopted by banks as well as other lending institutions, as it enables them to conduct both a quantitative as well as a qualitative measure and estimate of a borrower's creditworthiness.

Cash Flow

A borrower's cash flow is a measure of the amount of money remaining after deducting expenses as well as other debt-repayment obligations. This amount is usually what is left after a borrower spends their income on the various monthly obligations. A projection of the cash flow is therefore important, as it demonstrates and dissects a potential borrower's income against the expenditure, even giving a projection of the future. Thus, a person's cash flow projection in essence defines the person's eventual capacity in repaying a borrowed loan (Controller, n.d.). Consequently, lending institutions pay very close attention to a person's cash flow record before deciding the rate of interest to impose on the loan.

While it may be relatively easy and straightforward to determine a personal cash flow record for a short period of time, a majority of lending institutions require for a person or business to have a cash flow projection for up to three years ahead. The projections for businesses is a bit complicated since the lender ought to consider factors such as the earning prior to depreciation, interest, as well as amortization, often referred to as pro forma projections. In addition, lenders have to consider factors such as the minimum-debt-service-coverage ratio for businesses (minimum DSC). This ratio helps in evaluating if a business has any money left in its coffers after paying loans.

Credit or Character

In lending terms, character is popularly called credit history. This factor has been described to be as the most vital of the three C's. The reason behind this is because credit history of a person represents an overall reputation of a borrower regarding all available records pertaining to debt repayment. This requires a potential borrower to be honest regarding their debt-repayment history. Factors that are scrutinized by the lending institutions in this case are: if the borrower utilized the debts appropriately before, if they remit bills on time, how long one has lived in a current location, and what profession one held prior to the present business ("Three C's of Credit," n.d.). After considering all of these factors, the lenders usually assign a numerical grading that ranges form 300–850. The lower the score, the higher interest rate, and the higher the score, the lower the interest rate.

Collateral

A collateral is usually an asset that a borrower presents the lending institution to act as insurance in the case of loan default. Among the assets most considered for collateral are accounts receivable, inventory, equipment, and real estate. In cases where a borrower presents a lending institution with collateral, they are basically reducing the risk factor on the particular loans (Paisabazaar, 2016). Thus, a borrower who has valuable collateral often gets lower interest rates. The lending institutions, however, have to conduct valuations on the collateral to determine loan-to-value ratios.

Reference List

Controller, C., n.d. "The Three Cs of Lending: Cash Flow, Character, and Collateral," *Complete Controller*. URL https://www.completecontroller.com/the-three-cs-of-lending-cash-flow-character-and-collateral/ (accessed 11.25.19).

Paisabazaar, 2016, "The 3Cs of Credit Definition: Character, Capacity, Collateral," Comp. Apply Loans Credit Cards India- Paisabazaar.com. URL https://www.paisabazaar.com/credit-report/the-3cs-of-credit-reports-character-capacity-collateral/ (accessed 11.25.19).

"Three Cs of Credit," [WWW Document], n.d. URL https://www.firstcitizens.com/personal/advice/managing-credit/build-credit/three-c (accessed 11.25.19).

CHAPTER 6

THE THREE C'S OF FUNDING

Three C's. If you are considering getting funding, you need to know where you stand in terms of the three C's. It is what almost every lender, and funder, wants to see. The first C is credit, and it is an important part of how the lender will determine their risk in funding you. Many people look at credit as this ambiguous number that helps or hurts them with opportunity without understanding how a funder looks at your credit to determine their risk. I am a big fan of understanding things from different points of view in order to correctly respond in a way that will be most optimal for oneself. If you did not repay the last several organizations that extended you credit, then that tells me as a lender what type of risk there will be associated with lending to you.

The second C is cash flow. The second C is really important for the organization to determine whether or not you could afford the amount you are asking for. The first C as credit helps them make a judgement on whether or not you are willing to repay debt. The second C tells them if you are able to pay the debt. There are several documents that lenders and funders look at to determine your cash flow. The first document is one of the more controversial documents that has a love-hate relationship with many entrepreneurs. That is their business and personal taxes. The reason that this is so controversial is because almost every business tries to show they made less to lessen their tax burden. But when you need funding, lenders have to look at your taxes to determine your cash flow. They have to assume that many if not all those write-offs are justifiable and would still be needed. Profit and loss statements and balance sheets are the other documents that lenders use to see what the cash flow looks like.

The third and final C is collateral. Collateral is important because it says that the funder is not the only one taking the risk. When someone has collateral that they are putting into the loan, it tells the funder, "Not only am I telling you to take a risk on my business by lending me this amount but also I have something of value that I will use to demonstrate that I am committed to this value." There is a plethora of different collaterals that are looked at. I want to start with what is usually not considered. Many funders do not consider intellectual property. There could be many reasons why, but my opinion is that one would need to be a subject-matter expert in the area where the intellectual property is involved to determine the possible value of an intellectual property. I would like to address the only nonphysical asset that I have noticed many funders use as collateral: invoices. Many people consider collateral to only be real estate or equipment (which are the primary ones that is considered); however, invoices are often considered to provide factoring for some of the services that has been completed but not paid yet. On the accounting document that helps funders determine and be able to look at this, it is a document called the account receivable aging report, often referred to as AR report. This report details unpaid customer invoices.

Financial institutions are involved in the business of lending money to people with an aim of making profits from the charged interest. This is a risky business and the business has to do all that is possible to protect itself. To do this, financial institutions device strategies to use when lending to other businesses and individuals. These strategies are the three C's of funding, which include cash flow, character, and collateral.

Cash Flow

The cash flow of a business is used by lending institutions to determine the amount of loan and the repayment terms and conditions. The cash flow status of a business is determined by looking at the business's profit and loss accounts. According to Onyiriuba (2016, p. 394), profit and loss accounts is a statement of a company's revenue, expenditure, and profits for a period of a month, quarterly, semiannually, or annually.

To determine if a company or a business qualify for a loan, the cash flow must be strong and consistent. This means that through the profit and loss statements, the business must be able to demonstrate that it has been in business for a period of time and has been making profits while at it (Onyiriuba, 2016, p. 394). This flow of cash in a business is necessary, as some of the cash can be used for loan repayment. The lender has to understand the liquidity of the client before issuing the loans, as it will determine how they can faithfully repay the loan.

Character or Credit History

The character has to do with the credit history of an organization or a business. By generating a report of a borrower's credit history through three major bureaus—Experian, TransUnion, and Equifax— the lender is able to understand the eligibility of a borrower to repay the loan they are seeking (Bijak, Thomas, and Mues, 2014, p. 5). In this case, there are businesses or individuals who might default on loan repayment from one financial institution and then seek funding from another. This character or credit-history analysis helps to protect the lender from lending money to such businesses and individuals. The history of a client in loan repayment is crucial in determining their ability to pay future loans (Bijak, Thomas, and Mues, 2014, p. 15). A good track record in loan repayment means a good credit rating, which translates to the ability to acquire loans from financial institutions.

Collateral

A collateral in the loan business is a borrower's asset that is pledged against a loan to assure the lender that the borrower will be committed to the loan repayment (Dias Duarte, et al, 2017, p. 406). Business assets that can be used as collateral for a loan are analyzed by looking at the business's balance sheet. A balance sheet is a state-ment of the business's assets, liability, and shareholder's equity as at a particular time. The lender will require and up-to-date balance sheet of a business to understand the value of assets owned by a borrower, so as to determine if they qualify for a loan.

Collateral is important, as the lender is assured that should the worst-case scenario happen and the borrower default to repay the loan, the lender can recover collateral and liquidate as a repayment for the loans (Dias Duarte, et al, 2017, p. 417). The higher the collateral value, then the higher the loan a borrower can get and vice versa.

Reference List

Bijak, K., Thomas, L. C., and Mues, C., 2014, "Dynamic affordability assessment: predicting an applicant's ability to repay over the life of the loan," *The Journal of Credit Risk*, 10(1), 3–32. doi:10.21314/ jcr.2014.171

Dias Duarte, F., Matias Gama, A. P., and Paulo Esperança, J., 2017, "Collateral-based in SME lending: The role of business collateral and personal collateral in less-developed countries," *Research in International Business and Finance*, 39, 406–422. doi:10.1016/j. ribaf.2016.07.005

Onyiriuba, L. 2016, "Cash Flow Analysis and Lending to Corporate Borrowers," *Emerging Market Bank Lending and Credit Risk Control*, 393–417. doi:10.1016/b978-0-12-803438-5.00023-4

CHAPTER 7

DOCUMENTATION AND ITS CONNECTION TO THE INTEREST CHARGED

This chapter will aim to bridge the divide between the lender's perspective and the business owner's perspective while seeking funding in regard to documentation. We will discuss both the connection between documentation and interest charge as well as all the risk-mitigating ways that documentation helps support the lending business. I do know that the first part of this chapter will be of greater interest to those who are trying to nail down the connection between interest and documentation, and the second part will be of greater interest to those who are engrossed in how all the documentation will help mitigate risk in the business of lending.

The Connection between the Amount of Documentation Required and Interest Charged

The loans that usually require less documentation are usually more expensive loans. Many business owners are busy running their businesses and do not want to take an exorbitant amount of time completing documentation. Documentation is what funders use to determine the risk level. The risk level is what is used to determine the interest charged. Whenever you can get a loan with less documentation, it also means that the lender involved is willing to take higher-risk clients. It also means they prefer higher risk, because they are going to be charging more interest on those particular loans. Many characterized these lenders as sharks or some form of predator. But in reality, in a capitalistic society, businesses have a choice, and they weigh the pros and cons of their time. Some entrepreneurs decide to go with the more expensive loan for the convenience of not having to invest a considerable amount of time dedicated to gathering documentation; although some may regret that decision when they are in the process of repaying back the loan, but it was still a decision that the business owner makes in consideration of their unique circumstance.

I do not believe one loan is better than the other in abstract. I do believe that a business owner must objectively review the pros and cons of each decision based upon their situation and make it so that way it is a win-win scenario, even if that involves the business owner paying higher interest. Because of the demand for these types of loans and the expediency of getting the funding in a matter of days, Doriscar Capital Group do have funders that meet this criterion within its portfolio of financial products.

Documentation in the loan business is what funders use to determine a client's level of risk. The risk level is what is used to determine the interest charged (Berg, Saunders, and Steffen, 2016, pp. 1357–1392). The rest of this chapter will address documentation from a lender's perspective so that one can understand the reasoning and some of the facets of mitigating risk through documentation.

Mitigating Risk through Documentation in the Lending Business

A registered funding entity should create a working framework of managing risks and periodically examine the usefulness of that framework. Inner audit functionality can help a certified company to achieve its aims by bringing a systematic, disciplined method for assessing and continually improving the efficiency of its management of risks and internal control procedure. If a registered corporation has an inner audit function, the senior auditor should suit qualifications and have a direct-access line to the board or the panel audit group to convey the essential level of ability, autonomy, and neutrality to the role (Ibtissem and Bouri, 2013, pp. 9–24). If a registered entity lacks an inner audit function, the panel or audit group should examine periodically whether that function is needed.

The risk management systems of lending institutions are developed in assessing potential financial and other risks to its assets and operations and plan for their resiliencies (Murfin and Petersen, 2016, pp. 300–326). While decisions and reviews of capital investments integrate possible range of risks, it will be hard to forecast with confidence the severity, timing, or frequency of such occurrences, any of which might have substantial material negative effects on the firm's outcomes of financial conditions or operation without proper documentation. The supporting statements cited in the risk factor, the part

47

that is related to financial and economic risks, should show that the company has been transparent in reporting its risks.

Risk management is the structure, culture, and procedures that are directed toward taking advantage of possible opportunities while monitoring potential harmful threats (Berg, Saunders, and Steffen, 2016, pp. 1357–1392). The management of risks starts with comprehending the appetite of the perils. When borrowers question the time-consuming process of providing documentation, many do not consider the financial risk involved with the lending institution in the event of default.

The lending entities will be able to create a sound framework for risk assessment and management processes and occasionally review the framework effectiveness when proper documentation is provided. The principles of corporate governance will enable the board to set organizational risk appetite and then ensure it create a framework of risk management to assess and manage risks on an ongoing basis, which is why documentation is so important to lending institutions. The recommendations and principles of the corporate governance offer the benchmarks against which entities should evaluate and measure risk. With proper documentations, certain particular types of risk such as fraud are minimized (Ibtissem and Bouri, 2013, pp. 9–24). This implies that a funding company will be able to fill the loopholes that would otherwise lead to loss of the funding company's funds.

From internal documents to agreements with external parties, documentations touch all aspects of investing (Murfin and Petersen, 2016, pp. 300–326). Documentation also offers proof of how firms function and interact externally and internally to deliver their services. When processes, policies, and procedures are poorly documented or undocumented, there are rooms for doubts since the processes, policies, and procedures can be subject to undue influences or interpretations. Proper documentation is critical for investors because it eliminates ambiguity; They are important for investors because they enable the financers to understand whether the companies are operating according to corporate governance or not (Ibtissem and Bouri, 2013, pp. 9–24). Investors are ready to invest in firms with proper documentations because they feel that such businesses have less risks and it would be safe to invest in them.

Documentation shall minimize liabilities and mitigate risks from unforeseen events and lawsuits. It helps in resolving disputes within the organization (Berg, Saunders, and Steffen, 2016, pp. 1357–1392). Documentation outlines the wealth-distribution details and clearly describes the particular roles of company stakeholders such as the board of directors, the advisors, the employees, and the partners. Although the documentation that one is looking at is mainly for financial review, such as taxes, P and L Statements, and A and R statements. The documentation in this manner enables the investor or lender to make evidence-based investment decision.

Many businesses do not like to take away time from their core business to produce documentation when considering getting a loan. I just wanted to explain the importance of the documentation to the lender and inform borrowers that there is no right or wrong way in particular. But once you understand the importance of documentation to lenders, you will also understand why lenders that are willing to lend with less documentation has to charge (the responsible business decision) higher interest to compensate for missing out on the wealth of knowledge the documentation usually provides, in a way that would have limited the lending institution's risk.

In conclusion, these seven things one should know is important in helping businesses to better understand the lender's perspective. If one could understand how the lender is looking at a set of facts, it may be easier to predict how the lenders will act in certain situations. I believe there is enormous benefit for business owners and investors if they understand how lending institutions are likely to act in a given scenario. Being able to effectively anticipate how lending institutions may react with a given set of facts will empower businesses to employ effective strategies in their pursuit of reaching their lending needs. This book does not cover every facet of how a lender approaches a set of facts but aims to arm the reader with a perspective that I noticed wasn't prevalent among many businesses. For example, if one understands that most lending institutions are niche in nature of their funding choices, one could understand the benefit of working with an organization that works with several lending institutions with a variety of lending preferences. Many businesses assume that because one lender said no, that even though they have a viable business, they will not be able to find financing for their funding needs. The reality is that if you could afford the loan you are requesting, backed up by your business cash flow numbers, you may be able to find another lender that has a preference that is closer to your business profile.

Reference List

Berg, T., Saunders, A., and Steffen, S., 2016, "The total cost of corporate borrowing in the loan market: Don't ignore the fees," *The Journal of Finance*, 71(3), pp. 1357–1392.

Ibtissem, B. and Bouri, A., 2013, "Credit risk management in microfinance: The conceptual framework," *ACRN Journal of Finance and Risk Perspectives*, 2(1), pp. 9–24.

Murfin, J. and Petersen, M., 2016, "Loans on sale: Credit market seasonality, borrower need, and lender rents," *Journal of Financial Economics*, 121(2), pp. 300–326.

www.ingramcontent.com/pod-product-compliance
Lightning Source LLC
Chambersburg PA
CBHW010002190526
45157CB00017B/3286